TO REASON WHY

TO REASON WHY

Rose Basile Green

South Brunswick and New York:
A.S.Barnes and Company
London: Thomas Yoseloff Ltd

A.S. Barnes and Co., Inc.
Cranbury, New Jersey 08512

Thomas Yoseloff Ltd
108 New Bond Street
London WlY OQX, England

ISBN 0-498-01042-2
Printed in the United States of America

PREFACE

People everywhere are standing up to be counted. Women, for example, are insisting on the real as well as the legal deletion of discriminatory priorities in sex, race, religion, and nationality. In religion they are seeking to become persons as significant in the structure of the Church as they are becoming in the State.

At the opening of Vatican Council II, Pope John said, "In the daily exercise of our pastoral office, we sometimes have to listen . . . to voices of persons who . . . can see nothing but prevarication and ruin. . . . We feel we must disagree with those prophets of doom who are always forecasting disaster. . . . " In confronting this age of discord and dissent, many bishops and other Church administrators have asserted that it is their duty to give examples of unity and love, urging methods of criticism which will correct, reconcile, and unify rather than polarize, and will construct rather than destroy.

Within the frame of this constructive spirit seeking to evolve unity from diversification, the various questions in the following verses are offered for the clarification which dispels dissension or eventual loss of faith. In these sonnets the writer has chosen to refer to the materials of the Epistles and Gospels of the fifty-two Sundays of the traditional Roman Catholic Church year. Since Vatican Council II, the Church has reorganized the liturgy and its language, but the sources in **The New Testament*** remain unchanged. It is no secret, however, that at all times some of the parishioners of the Church have puzzled over the meanings of these sources. As the ministers of religion prepare their homilies to interpret the reconstructed liturgy, they might program answers to some of the questions which the faithful have been asking for generations. The questions posed here are current and pertinent in their insistence on the equal right of all persons to justice.

R.B.G.

*Based on **The New Testmanet** translated from the Latin Vulgate and first published by the English College at Rheims, A.D. 1582.

TO REASON WHY

FIRST SUNDAY of ADVENT

Epistle ROMANS 13:11–14

11   And that, knowing the season, that it is now the hour for us to rise from sleep. For now our salvation is nearer than when we believed.

12   The night is passed and the day is at hand. Let us therefore cast off the works of darkness and put on the armour of light.

13   Let us walk honestly, as in the day: not in rioting and drunkenness, not in chambering and impurities, not in contention and envy.

14   But put ye on the Lord Jesus Christ: and make not provision for the flesh in its concupiscences.

Gospel LUKE 21:25–33

25   And there shall be signs in the sun and in the moon and in the stars; and upon the earth distress of nations, by reason of the confusion of the roaring of the sea and of the waves:

26   Men withering away for fear and expectation of what shall come upon the whole world. For the powers of heaven shall be moved.

27   And then they shall see the Son of man coming in a cloud, with great power and majesty.

28   But when these things begin to come to pass, look up and lift up your heads, because your redemption is at hand.

29   And he spoke to them a similitude. See the fig tree and all the trees:

30   When they now shoot forth their fruit, you know that summer is nigh;

31   So you also, when you shall see these things come to pass, know that the kingdom of God is at hand.

32   Amen, I say to you, this generation shall not pass away till all things be fulfilled.

33   Heaven and earth shall pass away: but my words shall not pass away.

I

FIRST SUNDAY of ADVENT

At dawn the Word cloud-bursts the birth of man

And stirs him from his bare, vile sleep. The night

Is passed; the day awaits; the stars are wan

From battles with the dark. The signs are bright;

They frame the brewing fumes of chemistry,

All burning with the atoms in a dance

Of matter, nations in adversity,

Erasing heaven with the spew of chance,

To scorch the earth. They show the fruits of trees

Where partridges redeem the primal sound

And flush away the metal-withered leaves,

Untaping music, words where truth is bound.

But, if all things shall pass away, to know need I

Have come at all in pain to hear the Word and die?

II

SECOND SUNDAY of ADVENT

Epistle ROMANS 15:4—13

4 For what things soever were written were written for our learning: that, through patience and the comfort of the scriptures, we might have hope.

5 Now the God of patience and of comfort grant you to be of one mind, one towards another, according to Jesus Christ:

6 That with one mind and with one mouth you may glorify God and the Father of our Lord Jesus Christ.

7 Wherefore, receive one another, as Christ also hath received you, unto the honour of God.

9 But that the Gentiles are to glorify God for his mercy, as it is written: Therefore will I confess to thee, O Lord among the Gentiles and will sing to thy name.

10 And again he saith: Rejoice, ye Gentiles, with his people.

11 And again: Praise the Lord, all ye Gentiles: and magnify him, all ye people.

12 And again, Isaias saith: There shall be a root of Jesse; and he that shall rise up to rule the Gentiles, in him the Gentiles shall hope.

Gospel MATTHEW 11:2—10

2 Now when John had heard in prison the works of Christ, sending two of his disciples, he said to him:

3 Art thou he that are to come, or look we for another?

4 And Jesus making answer said to them: Go and relate to John what you have heard and seen.

5 The blind see, the lame walk, the lepers are cleansed, the deaf hear, the dead rise again, the poor have the gospel preached to them.

6 And blessed is he that shall not be scandalized in me.

7 And when they went their way, Jesus began to say to the multitudes concerning John: What went you out into the desert to see? A reed shaken with the wind?

8 But what went you out to see? A man clothed in soft garments? Behold they that are clothed in soft garments are in the house of kings.

9 But what went you out to see? A prophet? Yea, I tell you, and more than a prophet.

10 For this is he of whom it is written: Behold I send my angel before thy face, who shall prepare thy way before thee.

II

SECOND SUNDAY of ADVENT

The shadow is the sign of solid stuff,

The horoscope that prophesies the light.

It warns of thunder and of windy bluff,

Relieving blots where fusion blurs the sight.

The messenger with lines refracts the blind

And heals the lame of shame to walk again;

His music is no bending waft of wind

That wilts the reed with every changing rain.

His mansion has no regal silk, no seat

To fence the moving sands of prophecy;

But he has more to etch upon a face

That can reveal the Word, the way to see.

But if my busy vineyard is no desert land,

Should I, at work today, not hear the Word at ha

SUNDAY WITHIN the OCTAVE of CHRISTMAS

Epistle GALATIANS 4:1—7

Now I say: As long as the heir is a child, he differeth nothing from a servant, though he be Lord of all.

2 But is under tutors and governors until the time appointed by the father.

3 So we also, when we were children, were serving under the elements of the world.

4 But when the fulness of the time was come, God sent his Son, made of a woman, made under the law:

5 That he might redeem them who were under the law: that we might receive the adoption of sons.

6 And because you are sons, God hath sent the Spirit of his Son into your hearts, crying: Abba, Father.

7 Therefore, now he is not a servant, but a son. And if a son, an heir also through God.

Gospel LUKE 2:33-40

33 And his father and mother were wondering at those things which were spoken concerning him.

34 And Simeon blessed them and said to Mary his mother: Behold this child is set for the fall and for the resurrection of many in Israel and for a sign which shall be contradicted.

35 And thy own soul a sword shall pierce, that, out of many hearts thoughts may be revealed.

36 And there was one Anna, a prophetess, the daughter of Phanuel; of the tribe of Aser. She was far advanced in years and had lived with her husband seven years from her virginity.

37 And she was a widow until fourscore and four years; who departed not from the temple, by fastings and prayers serving night and day.

38 Now she, at the same hour, coming in, confessed to the Lord: and spoke of him to all that looked for the redemption of Israel.

39 And after they had performed all things according to the law of the Lord, they returned into Galilee, to their city Nazareth.

40 And the child grew and waxed strong, full of wisdom: and the grace of God was in him.

III

SUNDAY BETWEEN CHRISTMAS AND NEW YEAR

The Word is born and then it starts to be;

The birth comes first and then the being is.

The light is swaddled in the dark, and he

Is bedded in the frame whose grain is his;

For there the pages blank are staring wide,

Blanched mute in wonder at this bread with voice

That hence will spill the message to decide

The verses, wine to urge that all rejoice.

The husband is the life outside the Word,

In darkness ploughing not the planted seed.

The wife, whose womb from Else's message heard,

Receives the sound and syncopates its need.

Why, then, the woman who first birthed and reared the Word

Must guard in silence all that she has done and heard?

SUNDAY of the EPIPHANY

Epistle ISAIAS 60:1—6

Gospel MATTHEW 2:1-12

When Jesus therefore was born in Bethlehem of Juda, in the days of king Herod, behold, there came wise men from the east to Jerusalem,

2   Saying, Where is he that is born king of the Jews? For we have seen his star in the east, and are come to adore him.

3   And king Herod hearing this was troubled, and all Jerusalem with him.

4   And assembling together all the chief priests and the scribes of the people, he inquired of them where Christ should be born.

5   But they said to him: In Bethlehem of Juda. For so it is written by the prophet:

6   And thou Bethlehem the land of Juda art not the least among the princes of Juda: for out of thee shall come forth the captain that shall rule my people Israel.

7   Then Herod privately calling the wise men, learned diligently of them the time of the star which appeared to them.

8   And sending them into Bethlehem, said: Go and diligently inquire after the child, and when you have found him, bring me word again, that I also may come and adore him.

9   Who having heard the king went their way; and behold the star which they had seen in the east went before them until it came and stood over where the child was.

10   And seeing the star they rejoiced with exceeding great joy.

11   And entering into the house, they found the child with Mary his mother. And falling down they adored him. And opening their treasures, they offered him gifts: gold, frankincense, and myrrh.

12   And having received an answer in sleep that they should not return to Herod, they went back another way into their country.

IV

SUNDAY of the EPIPHANY

There comes a time when one must see the Word

And follow west the homing of its star,

For vision manifests the sound he heard

Where darkness was. Now light is here and far.

The gold and frankincense of Saba rise

As lightning sparks the voiced eternity;

And from the East flame up the purple wise

To ground the ash and sun the mystery.

The lie would flesh to-day a bull-penned king,

That it might blot the God-birthed telling ray;

But the dream bears light, the sight the Word will bring

To each, the dreamer reaching for the way.

Why, then, the glare of profit gold, so flashed today,

By blinding men with wealth can still the Word betray?

FIRST SUNDAY AFTER the EPIPHANY

Epistle COLOSSIANS 3:12-17

12   Put ye on therefore, as the elect of God, holy and beloved, the bowels of mercy, benignity, humility, modesty, patience:

14   But above all these things have charity, which is the bond of perfection.

16   Let the word of Christ dwell in you abundantly: in all wisdom, teaching and admonishing one another in psalms, hymns and spiritual canticles, singing in grace in your hearts to God.

17   All whatsoever you do in word or in work, do all in the name of the Lord Jesus Christ, giving thanks to God and the Father by him.

Gospel LUKE 2:42-52

42   And when he was twelve years old, they going up into Jerusalem, according to the custom of the feast,

43   And having fulfilled the days, when they returned, the child Jesus remained in Jerusalem. And his parents knew it not.

44   And thinking that he was in the company, they came a day's journey and sought him among their kinsfolks and acquaintance.

45   And not finding him, they returned into Jerusalem, seeking him.

46   And it came to pass that, after three days, they found him in the temple, sitting in the midst of the doctors, hearing them and asking them questions.

47   And all that heard him were astonished at his wisdom and his answers.

48   And seeing him, they wondered. And his mother said to him: Son, why hast thou done so to us? Behold thy father and I have sought thee sorrowing.

49   And he said to them: How is it that you sought me? Did you not know that I must be about my father's business?

50   And they understood not the word that he spoke unto them.

51   And he went down with them and came to Nazareth and was subject to them. And his mother kept all these words in her heart.

52   And Jesus advanced in wisdom and age and grace with God and men.

V

FIRST SUNDAY AFTER the EPIPHANY

We find no peace in relatives and friends,

For neither hearth nor tavern shelters us

In permanence. The homing table ends

With fabricated dreams, no omnibus

To starry highways washed away by storm,

No stairways to the choir of our songs.

The trio of our days now tests our form

To seek the temple where each one belongs.

The father's business, the nothing, all,

Cements the crowded avenues of fairs.

We hear the rushing of each rise and fall

Of markets dealing hard with human wares.

But, should the chosen son disdain his mother's word

Within the public temple where her dream is stirred?

SECOND SUNDAY AFTER the EPIPHANY

Epistle ROMANS 12:6—16

Gospel JOHN 2:1—11

1   And the third day, there was a marriage in Cana of Galilee: and the mother of Jesus was there.

2   And Jesus also was invited, and his disciples, to the marriage.

3   And the wine failing, the mother of Jesus saith to him: They have no wine.

4   And Jesus saith to her: Woman, what is that to me and to thee? My hour is not yet come.

5   His mother saith to the waiters: Whatsoever he shall say to you, do ye.

6   Now there were set there six waterpots of stone, according to the manner of the purifying of the Jews, containing two or three measures apiece.

7   Jesus saith to them: Fill the waterpots with water. And they filled them up to the brim.

8   And Jesus saith to them: Draw out **now** and carry to the chief steward of the feast. And they carried it.

9   And when the chief steward had tasted the water made wine and knew not whence it was, but the waiters knew who had drawn the water: the chief steward calleth the bridegroom,

10   And saith to him: Every man at first setteth forth good wine, and when men have well drunk, then that which is worse. But thou hast kept the good wine until now.

11   This beginning of miracles did Jesus in Cana of Galilee and manifested his glory. And his disciples believed in him.

VI

SECOND SUNDAY AFTER the EPIPHANY

"What wouldst thou have me do, woman," said he

As though she were attending at the hour;

But she endured, and "Do whatever He

Tells you," she said, and watered well the flower.

And, when at last the fruit distilled to wine,

There was enough for every guest to draw,

That each might sip or drink his fill to dine

With proper feasting for the wedding law.

And so, with his own gift each fills a jar

To draw the harvest when it caps the brim;

And then it follows that his chosen star

Transcends the clay that once had pottered him.

But, did the wine thus follow from the son's own deed,

Or was it from the mother's knowing of its need?

THIRD SUNDAY AFTER the EPIPHANY

Epistle ROMANS 12:16—21

Gospel MATTHEW 8:1—13

And when he was come down from the mountain, great multitudes followed him.

2   And behold a leper came and adored him, saying: Lord, if thou wilt, thou canst make me clean.

3   And Jesus stretching forth his hand, touched him, saying: I will. Be thou made clean. And forthwith his leprosy was cleansed.

4   And Jesus saith to him: See thou tell no man: but go, shew thyself to the priest and offer the gift which Moses commanded for a testimony unto them.

5   And when he had entered into Capharnaum, there came to him a centurion, beseeching him,

6   And saying: Lord, my servant lieth at home sick of the palsy and is grievously tormented.

7   And Jesus saith to him: I will come and heal him.

8   And the centurion making answer, said: Lord, I am not worthy that thou shouldst enter under my roof: but only say the word and my servant shall be healed.

9   For I also am a man subject to authority, having under me soldiers; and I say to this, Go, and he goeth, and to another, Come, and he cometh, and to my servant, Do this, and he doeth it.

10   And Jesus hearing this, marvelled and said to them that followed him: Amen, I say to you, I have not found so great faith in Israel.

11   And I say to you that many shall come from the east and the west, and shall sit down with Abraham and Isaac and Jacob in the kingdom of heaven:

12   But the children of the kingdom shall be cast out into the exterior darkness. There, shall be weeping and gnashing of teeth.

13   And Jesus said to the centurion: Go, and as thou hast believed so be it done to thee. And the servant was healed at the same hour.

THIRD SUNDAY AFTER the EPIPHANY

Let me not avenge the evil rendered me,

For brief is happiness that vengeance fires;

Its flame of satisfaction is not free

To last. It drops its ashes in the mires.

My hungry enemy will gorge my food,

And when he thirsts he sponges my best wine;

And he, a leper, is made clean and good,

While silence is the mercy which is mine.

The man of many words stirs up a wind

To dry the rivulets which flow from rain;

The man of action guards the broken bind

And shields him in the numbness of his pain.

Is not the Word, then, crippled by one tribe's loose talk,

While another's mute lieutenant makes the message walk?

FOURTH SUNDAY AFTER the EPIPHANY

Epistle ROMANS 13:8—10

8   Owe no man any thing, but to love one another. For he that loveth his neighbour hath fulfilled the law.

9   For: Thou shalt not commit adultery: Thou shalt not kill: Thou shalt not steal: Thou shalt not bear false witness: Thou shalt not covet. And if there be any other commandment, it is comprised in this word: Thou shalt love thy neighbour as thyself.

10   The love of our neighbour worketh no evil. Love therefore is the fulfilling of the law.

Gospel MATTHEW 8:23-27

23   And when he entered into the boat, his disciples followed him.

24   And behold a great tempest arose in the sea, so that the boat was covered with waves but he was asleep.

25   And they came to him and awaked him, saying: Lord, save us, we perish.

26   And Jesus saith to them: Why are you fearful, O ye of little faith? Then rising up he commanded the winds and the sea: and there came a great calm.

27   But the men wondered saying: What manner of man is this, for the winds and the sea obey him?

VIII

FOURTH SUNDAY AFTER the EPIPHANY

My weakness is too nude for me, alone,

To know the Word. I must know how it binds

My neighbor and his own, his every stone,

To me. His love for me the secret finds,

Forbidding me to steal, to lust, to take

As mine his time and name. Despite the storm

Which splinters rafts with waves that rock reefs break,

The Word in sleep still banks a conscience warm.

The sleep, the magic of our earthly things,

Is all the insulation of our fears;
And when we wake the restoration brings
The Word that calms the little faith of years.

And, yet, is not the earth the sleep that dreams the Word
That It above the waves and winds by all be heard?

FIFTH SUNDAY AFTER the EPIPHANY

Epistle COLOSSIANS 3:12–17

12   Put ye on therefore, as the elect of God, holy and beloved, the bowels of mercy, benignity, humility, modesty, patience:

13   Bearing with one another and forgiving one another, if any have a complaint against another. Even as the Lord hath forgiven you, so do you also.

14   But above all these things have charity, which is the bond of perfection.

15   And let the peace of Christ rejoice in your hearts, wherein also you are called in one body. And be ye thankful.

16   Let the word of Christ dwell in you abundantly: in all wisdom, teaching and admonishing one another in psalms, hymns and spiritual canticles, singing in grace in your hearts to God.

17   All whatsoever you do in word or in work, do all in the name of the Lord Jesus Christ, giving thanks to God and the Father by him.

Gospel MATTHEW 13:24-30

24   Another parable he proposed to them, saying: The kingdom of heaven is likened to a man that sowed good seed in his field.

25   But while men were asleep, his enemy came and oversowed cockle among the wheat and went his way.

26   And when the blade was sprung up and had brought forth fruit, then appeared also the cockle.

27   And the servants of the goodman of the house coming said to him: Sir, didst thou not sow good seed in thy field? Whence then hath it cockle?

28   And he saith to them: An enemy hath done this. And the servants said to him: Wilt thou that we go and gather it up?

29   And he said: No, lest perhaps gathering up the cockle, you root up the wheat also together with it.

30   Suffer both to grow until the harvest, and in the time of the harvest, I will say to the reapers: Gather up first the cockle and bind it into bundles to burn, but the wheat gather ye into my barn.

IX

FIFTH SUNDAY AFTER the EPIPHANY

The weed of evil is a mystery.

While fretting at the roof of every good,

The weed-seed mutely fertilizes, free,

In careful grain. The farmer there has stood

In showers, seminating deep the soil

Where patience tends the stems of charity,

Unbending evil by his daily toil

To prune and ripen fruit abundantly.

And so the seed not planted in the field

Together with the wheat is left to grow;

And when the reapers gather up the yield,

They burn the weeds the farmer did not sow.

But, if, while growing, then the weed destroys the grain,

What is the seed that should have nurtured in the rain?

SIXTH SUNDAY AFTER the EPIPHANY

Epistle THESSALONIANS 1:2–10

2   Grace be to you and peace. We give thanks to God always for you all: making remembrance of you in our prayers without ceasing.

3   Being mindful of the work of your faith and labour and charity: and of the enduring of the hope of our Lord Jesus Christ before God and our Father.

4   Knowing, brethren, beloved of God, your election:

5   For our gospel hath not been unto you in word only, but in power also; and in the Holy Ghost and in much fulness, as you know what manner of men we have been among you for your sakes.

6   And you became followers of us and of the Lord: receiving the word in much tribulation, with joy of the Holy Ghost:

7   So that you were made a pattern to all that believe in Macedonia and in Achaia.

8   For from you was spread abroad the word of the Lord not only in Macedonia and in Achaia but also in every place: your faith which is towards God is gone forth, so that we need not to speak any thing.

Gospel MATTHEW 13:31-35

31   Another parable he proposed unto them, saying: The kingdom of heaven is like to a grain of mustard seed which a man took and sowed in his field.

32   Which is the least indeed of all seeds: but when it is grown up, it is greater than all herbs and becometh a tree, so that the birds of the air come and dwell in the branches thereof.

33   Another parable he spoke to them: The kingdom of heaven is like to leaven which a woman took and hid in three measures of meal, until the whole was leavened.

34   All these things Jesus spoke in parables to the multitudes: and without parables he did not speak to them.

35   That it might be fulfilled which was spoken by the prophet, saying: I will open my mouth in parables, I will utter things hidden from the foundation of the world.

X

SIXTH SUNDAY AFTER the EPIPHANY

Look not for truth within the Word alone;

The strength to show and win in power lies.

The spirit dresses both the flesh and bone

With verbal armies that no foe defies.

From Macedonia and Achaia, through

All Rome is sound that brave Columbia hears;

The first atomic beep with ages grew;

The swell now grounds the music for the spheres.

As ready soil to birth the mustard seed,

To feed the flowered forests, branching naves,

So tripled measures now the choirs heed

And tape one note to modulate the waves.

And when the man thus sows the seed within the field,

Must not the woman make the leaven for the yield?

SEPTUAGESIMA SUNDAY

Epistle 1 CORINTHIANS 9:24–27; 10, 1–5

Gospel MATTHEW 20:1–16

The kingdom of heaven is like to an householder who went out early in the morning to hire labourers into his vineyard.

2   And having agreed with the labourers for a penny a day, he sent them into his vineyard.

3   And going out about the third hour, he saw others standing in the market place idle.

4   And he said to them: Go you also into my vineyard and I will give you what shall be just.

5   And they went their way. And again he went out about the sixth and the ninth hour and did in like manner.

6   But about the eleventh hour he went out and found others standing. And he saith to them: Why stand you here all the day idle?

7   They say to him: Because no man hath hired us. He saith to them: Go you also into my vineyard.

8   And when evening was come, the lord of the vineyard saith to his steward: Call the labourers and pay them their hire, beginning from the last even to the first.

9   When therefore they were come that came about the eleventh hour, they received every man a penny.

10   But when the first also came, they thought that they should receive more: and they also received every man a penny.

11   And receiving it they murmured against the master of the house.

12   Saying: These last have worked but one hour: and thou hast made them equal to us that have borne the burden of the day and the heats.

13   But he answering said to one of them: Friend, I do thee no wrong. Didst thou not agree with me for a penny?

14   Take what is thine and go thy way. I will also give to this last even as to thee.

15   Or, is it not lawful for me to do what I will? Is thy eye evil, because I am good?

16   So shall the last be first and the first last. For many are called but few chosen.

SEPTUAGESIMA SUNDAY

Of all who drink and eat the master's rock

The chosen few must race and realize

That for them all there is no common stock

And only one must live to win the prize.

"I do thee no injustice," says the Lord,

"For I with you a bargain fair have made.

You envy, then, my ledger and my sword;

But I have chosen who shall host my blade."

Reward of work is paralleled and won

By him who pearls the meadow at the dawn

And him who stirs the dust when sets the sun.

There is no measure to the use of brawn.

But, when the first is last and gives the last his seat,

Is he not like an ace reversed into retreat?

XII

SEXAGESIMA SUNDAY

Epistle 2 CORINTHIANS 11:19-33; 12:1—9

Gospel LUKE 8:4—15

4   And when a very great multitude was gathered together and hastened out of the cities, unto him, he spoke by a similitude.

5   The sower went out to sow his seed. And as he sowed, some fell by the way side. And it was trodden down: and the fowls of the air devoured it.

6   And other some fell upon a rock, and as soon as it was sprung up, it withered away, because it had no moisture.

7   And other some fell among thorns. And the thorns growing up with it, choked it.

8   And other some fell upon good ground and, being sprung up, yielded fruit a hundredfold. Saying these things, he cried out: He that hath ears to hear, let him hear.

9   And his disciples asked him what this parable might be.

10   To whom he said: To you it is given to know the mystery of the kingdom of God; but to the rest in parables, that seeing they may not see and hearing may not understand.

11   Now the parable is this: The seed is the word of God.

12   And they by the way side are they that hear: then the devil cometh and taketh the word out of their heart, lest believing they should be saved.

13   Now they upon the rock are they who when they hear receive the word with joy: and these have no roots; for they believe for a while and in time of temptation they fall away.

14   And that which fell among thorns are they who have heard and, going their way, are choked with the cares and riches and pleasures of this life and yield no fruit.

15   But that on the **good ground** are they who in a good and perfect heart, hearing the word, keep it and bring forth fruit in patience.

30

XII

SEXAGESIMA SUNDAY

Let me sink and wallow in infirmities

That I may know the timbre of my strength;

For secret words beyond Eumenides

Have sung the width of heaven and its length;

And in the depth and slough the seed upheaves

That it be lost and trodden under foot,

While sterile rock the stumbling bud receives

That it may seminate but take no root.

You see the seed fall dead among the thorns

Of cares that choke the breath of working corps.

For them no victory bugles and no horns;

For them lies scorched the earth of every war.

But, what is patience for the right, the just, the good,

When seed held fast by marplots ripens into food?

31

XIII

QUINQUAGESIMA SUNDAY

Epistle 1 CORINTHIANS 13:1—13

Gospel LUKE 18:31—43

31   Then Jesus took unto him the twelve and said to them: Behold, we go up to Jerusalem; and all things shall be accomplished which were written by the prophets concerning the Son of man.

32   For he shall be delivered to the Gentiles and shall be mocked and scourged and spit upon.

33   And after they have scourged him, they will put him to death. And the third day he shall rise again.

34   And they understood none of these things, and this word was hid from them: and they understood not the things that were said.

35   Now it came to pass, when he drew nigh to Jericho, that a certain blind man sat by the way side, begging.

36   And when he heard the multitude passing by, he asked what this meant.

37   And they told him that Jesus of Nazareth was passing by.

38   And he cried out, saying: Jesus Son of David, have mercy on me.

39   And they that went before rebuked him, that he should hold his peace; but he cried out much more: Son of David, have mercy on me.

40   And Jesus standing, commanded him to be brought unto him. And when he was come near, he asked him.

41   Saying: What wilt thou that I do to thee? But he said: Lord, that I may see.

42   And Jesus said to him: Receive thy sight: thy faith hath made thee whole.

43   And immediately he saw and followed him, glorifying God. And all the people when they saw it, gave praise to God.

XIII

QUINQUAGESIMA SUNDAY

The all we know is little and in part,

And that which we can prophesy is less;

But tongues will cease and prophecies depart

When knowledge, thus interred, will have no stress.

Though in a child the mind imperfect flays,

The mind in man with him comes face to face;

And then he puts away his infant ways

And tries the perfect image to embrace.

No tripled warnings light uncharted roads

Where blind men beg for mercy and for right;

The message of the passing Word forbodes

That anguish dies before the cry for sight.

But, why, in social acts of work and charity

The manner mild is taken for stupidity?

FIRST SUNDAY IN LENT

Epistle 2 CORINTHIANS 6:1—10

Gospel MATTHEW 4:1—11

1 Then Jesus was led by the spirit into the desert to be tempted by the devil.

2 And when he had fasted forty days and forty nights, afterwards he was hungry.

3 And the tempter coming said to him: If thou be the Son of God, command that these stones be made bread.

4 Who answered and said: It is written. Not in bread alone doth man live, but in every word that proceedeth from the mouth of God.

5 Then the devil took him up into the holy city and set him upon the pinnacle of the temple.

6 And said to him: If thou be the Son of God, cast thyself down, it is written: That he hath given his angels charge over thee, and in their hands shall they bear thee up, lest perhaps thou dash thy foot against a stone.

7 Jesus said to him: It is written gain: Thou shalt not tempt the Lord thy God.

8 Again the devil took him up into a very high mountain and shewed him all the kingdoms of the world and the glory of them.

9 And said to him: All these will I give thee, if falling down thou wilt adore me.

10 Then Jesus saith to him: Begone, Satan! For it is written: The Lord thy God shalt thou dore, and him only shalt thou serve.

11 Then the devil left him. And behold angels came and ministered to him.

XIV

FIRST SUNDAY IN LENT

I will not to my temptor give offence

And free him, thus, to blight my ministry;

Both right and left my armour gives defense

Against the bramble and the forestry.

And, though he hoist me to the highest bough,

Defying branches that might ease me down,

I take the fall to touch the treeless slough

Surrounding both the tavern and the town.

The desert there has forty wells of wine

Beneath the crusted asp and basilisk;

And noonday devils have no bread of mine;

They hear the Word and take no further risk.

But, if by bread alone my neighbor wants to live,

Must I delete the wine that I so freely give?

SECOND SUNDAY IN LENT

Epistle 1 THESSALONIANS 4:1—7

1   For the rest therefore, brethren, we pray and beseech you in the Lord Jesus that, as you have received from us, how you ought to walk and to please God, so also you would walk, that you may abound the more.

2   For you know what precepts I have given to you by the Lord Jesus.

3   For this is the will of God, your sanctification: That you should abstain from fornication:

6   And that no man overreach nor circumvent his brother in business: because the Lord is the avenger of all these things, as we have told you before and have testified.

7   For God hath not called us unto uncleanness, but unto sanctification.

Gospel MATTHEW 17:1—9

1   And after six days, Jesus taketh unto him Peter and James, and John his brother, and bringeth them up into a high mountain apart.

2   And he was transfigured before them. And his face did shine as the sun: and his garments became white as snow.

3   And behold there appeared to them Moses and Elias talking with him.

4   And Peter answering, said to Jesus: Lord, it is good for us to be here: if thou wilt, let us make here three tabernacles, one for thee, and one for Moses, and one for Elias.

5   And as he was yet speaking, behold a bright cloud overshadowed them. And lo, a voice out of the cloud, saying: This is my beloved Son in whom I am well pleased. Hear ye him.

6   And the disciples hearing, fell upon their face and were very much afraid.

7   And Jesus came and touched them and said to them: Arise, and fear not.

8   And they lifting up their eyes saw no one but only Jesus.

9   And as they came down from the mountain, Jesus charged them, saying: Tell the vision to no man till the Son of man be risen from the dead.

XV

SECOND SUNDAY IN LENT

In me waits full the well of holiness

From which the flow seeps out to me the ten,

The rivers, feeding seas of loneliness,

Transcending oceans, in their thirst for men.

My brothers climb the mountain just behind

The snow-capped tip where slip-streams write the Word,

The ten-fold law transfiguring the mind

Which in three ages history has heard.

Now "This is my beloved" is the ink,

Erasing visions of a penciled truth,

The epic resurrecting to the brink

What once was only verse, a thrust of youth.

Since death entombs the love which every mind enfolds,

Was not the light of truth eclipsed by other scrolls?

37

THIRD SUNDAY IN LENT

Epistle EPHESIANS 5:1-9

Gospel LUKE 11:14–28

14   And he was casting out a devil: and the same was dumb. And when he had cast out the devil, the dumb spoke: and the multitudes were in admiration at it.

15   But some of them said: He casteth out devils by Beelzebub, the prince of devils.

16   And others tempting, asked of him a sign from heaven.

17   But he seeing their thoughts, said to them: Every kingdom divided against itself shall be brought to desolation, and house upon house shall fall.

18   And if Satan also be divided against himself, how shall his kingdom stand? Because you say that through Beelzebub I cast out devils.

19   Now if I cast out devils by Beelzebub, by whom do your children cast them out? Therefore, they shall be your judges.

20   But if I by the finger of God cast out devils, doubtless the kingdom of God is come upon you.

21   When a strong man armed keepeth his court, those things are in peace which he possesseth.

22   But if a stronger than he come upon him and overcome him, he will take away all his armour wherein he trusted and will distribute his spoils.

23   He that is not with me is against me; and he that gathereth not with me scattereth.

24   When the unclean spirit is gone out of a man, he walketh through places without water, seeking rest; and not finding, he saith: I will return into my house whence I came out.

25   And when he is come, he findeth it swept and garnished.

26   Then he goeth and taketh with him seven other spirits more wicked than himself: and entering in they dwell there. And the last state of that man becomes worse than the first.

27   And it came to pass, as he spoke these things, a certain woman from the crowd, lifting up her voice, said to him: Blessed is the womb that bore thee and the paps that gave thee suck.

28   But he said: Yea rather, blessed are they who hear the word of God and keep it.

XVI

THIRD SUNDAY IN LENT

The word dissolves the evil on my tongue;

My silence suddenly articulates;

The speaker of the dreams has slowly wrung

The syllable that system speculates.

No spinning sounds shall lead the ear astray

To muff the drum where once the darkness stood;

Since light of self arrests the tri-staved fray,

I must explode the quiet of the wood;

For when the evil saturates the place

Where water never fed nor cleansed the sands,

It seeks with seven others to retrace

The sources it will dry with new demands.

Were not the womb and breast first blessed, before the Word

Could penetrate the ear in order to be heard?

FOURTH SUNDAY IN LENT

Epistle GALATIANS 4:22—31

Gospel JOHN 6:1—15

1 'After these things Jesus went over the sea of Galilee, which is that of Tiberias.

2 And a great multitude followed him, because they saw the miracles which he did on them that were diseased.

3 Jesus therefore went up into a mountain: and there he sat with his disciples.

4 Now the pasch, the festival day of the Jews, was near at hand.

5 When Jesus therefore had lifted up his eyes and seen that a very great multitude cometh to him, he said to Philip: Whence shall we buy bread, that these may eat?

6 And this he said to try him: for he himself knew what he would do.

7 Philip answered him: Two hundred pennyworth of bread is not sufficient for them, that every one may take a little.

8 One of his disciples, Andrew, the brother of Simon Peter, saith to him:

9 There is a boy here that hath five barley loaves and two fishes. But what are these among so many?

10 Then Jesus said: Make the men sit down. Now, there was much grass in the place. The men therefore sat down, in number about five thousand.

11 And Jesus took the loaves: and when he had given thanks, he distributed to them that were set down. In like manner also of the fishes, as much as they would.

12 And when they were filled, he said to his disciples: Gather up the fragments that remain, lest they be lost.

13 They gathered up therefore and filled twelve baskets with the fragments of the five barley loaves which remained over and above to them that had eaten.

14 Now those men, when they had seen what a miracle Jesus had done, said: This is of a truth the prophet that is to come into the world.

15 Jesus therefore, when he knew that they would come to take him by force and make him king, fled again into the mountains, himself alone.

FOURTH SUNDAY IN LENT

Beyond the wood I see the arc of light,

The azimuth from cave to solar dome;

Since Sinai still with Agar now will fight

Dividing issue of the street and home,

We, then, the old Tiberius must seek,

To find the matrix of fraternity,

Where two is five is twelve to feed the meek

Who need to search their lost maternity.

The preachers, mouthing primacy of sound,

Are brothers who divide the realm of home;

The discipline of self they have not found,

Who have not reasoned with the voice of Rome.

Why do we now reverse the law, betray the Word;

The slave be free, the free be slave, no reason heard?

PASSION SUNDAY

Epistle HEBREWS 9:11—15

Gospel JOHN 8:46-59

46   Which of you shall convince me of sin? If I say the truth to you, why do you not believe me?

47   He that is of God heareth the words of God. Therefore you hear them not, because you are not of God.

48   The Jews therefore answered and said to him: Do not we say well that thou art a Samaritan and hast a devil?

49   Jesus answered: I have not a devil: but I honour my Father. And you have dishonoured me.

50   But I seek not my own glory: there is one that seeketh and judgeth.

51   Amen, amen, I say to you: If any man keep my word, he shall not see death for ever.

52   The Jews therefore said: Now we know that thou hast a devil. Abraham is dead and the prophets; and thou sayest: If any man keep my word, he shall not taste death for ever.

53   Art thou greater than our father Abraham who is dead? And the prophets are dead. Whom dost thou make thyself?

54   Jesus answered: If I glorify myself, my glory is nothing. It is my Father that glorifieth me, of whom you say that he is your God.

55   And you have not known him: but I know him. And if I shall say that I know him not, I shall be like to you, a liar. But I do know him and do keep his word.

56   Abraham your father rejoiced that he might see my day: he saw it and was glad.

57   The Jews therefore said to him: Thou art not yet fifty years old. And hast thou seen Abraham?

58   Jesus said to them: Amen, amen, I say to you, before Abraham was made, I am.

59   They took up stones therefore to cast at him. But Jesus hid himself and went out of the temple.

XVIII

PASSION SUNDAY

The young cram out to strike all crowns with stones;

They kneel and shriek; blue veins are bleeding red.

Where once they firmed their flesh with bullied bones,

Their martyred goats now rot among the dead.

Only the mind can weigh the blood of man

To clear the conscience for eternity,

Discarding flesh from where division ran

That gave to time a marked paternity.

"It is my Father glorying me," is clear;

And with the timelessness of time, "I am."

The Word falls straight upon the drum-tapped ear

And rolls the sound to every Abraham.

But, when was not the time when all the Word could hear,

And first was Caesar's wife who tuned to him her ear?

XIX

PALM SUNDAY

Epistle PHILIPPIANS 2:5-11

5   For let this mind be in you, which was also in Christ Jesus:

6   Who being in the form of God, thought it not robbery to be equal with God:

7   But emptied himself, taking the form of a servant, being made in the likeness of men, and in habit found as a man.

8   He humbled himself, becoming obedient unto death, even to the death of the cross.

9   For which cause, God also hath exalted him and hath given him a name which is above all names:

10   That in the name of Jesus every knee should bow, of those that are in heaven, on earth, and under the earth:

11   And that every tongue should confess that the Lord Jesus Christ is in the glory of God the Father.

Gospel MATTHEW 27:45—52

45   Now from the sixth hour, there was darkness over the whole earth, until the ninth hour.

46   And about the ninth hour, Jesus cried with a loud voice, saying: Eli, Eli, lamma sabacthani? That is, My God, My God, why hast thou forsaken me?

47   And some that stood there and heard said: This man calleth Elias.

48   And immediately one of them running took a sponge and filled it with vinegar and put it on a reed and gave him to drink.

49   And the others said: Let be. Let us see whether Elias will come to deliver him.

50   And Jesus again crying with a loud voice, yielded up the ghost.

51   And behold the veil of the temple was rent in two from the top even to the bottom: and the earth quaked and the rocks were rent.

52   And the graves were opened: and many bodies of the saints that had slept arose.

44

XIX

PALM SUNDAY

The branch of palm now frets for victory

To cut the throats that shout for cross and blood,

Not knowing that their page in history

Is wheel-turned hence by a diurnal flood.

The horns of unicorns lie tense and low

To spring and pierce the empty God in man;

In stealth the killing hand no blood will show,

But screens behind the riots it will fan.

Look at that frenzied mob of sweating lust,

Rejecting tripled pacts of bread and wine,

Before them reason washes blame with trust

That silver be for man a thorn divine.

Just man, does not the dream give to the Word its home

When suffered for Him by the pleading wife of Rome?

45

XX

EASTER SUNDAY

Epistle 1 CORINTHIANS 5:7—8

7   Purge out the old leaven, that you may be a new paste, as you are unleavened. For Christ our pasch is sacrificed.

8   Therefore, let us feast, not with the old leaven, nor with the leaven of malice and wickedness: but with the unleavened bread of sincerity and truth.

Gospel MARK 16:1—7

1   And when the sabbath was past, Mary Magdalen and Mary the mother of James and Salome bought sweet spices, that coming, they might anoint Jesus.

2   And very early in the morning, the first day of the week, they come to the sepulchre, the sun being now risen.

3   And they said one to another: Who shall roll us back the stone from the door of the sepulchre?

4   And looking, they saw the stone rolled back. For it was very great.

5   And entering into the sepulchre, they saw a young man sitting on the right side, clothed with a white robe: and they were astonished.

6   Who saith to them: Be not affrighted. You seek Jesus of Nazareth, who was crucified. He is risen: he is not here. Behold the place where they laid him.

7   But go, tell his disciples and Peter that he goeth before you into Galilee. There you shall see him, as he told you.

XX

EASTER SUNDAY

In resurrection is the way of life

By which immortal reason has no end;

Since from the ashes charred by burning strife

The mind restores what bodied tricks defend.

In truth there is no void, no death, no line;

But it must lie unleavened for a purge,

That I may be a dough renewed for wine;

A pristine faith, which must be lost to urge

The struggle to the real in the divine,

Was born within the silence of the womb

That parturated first the godly sign,

Then voiced its time by breaking from the tomb.

And as the tomb rebirths the tree-hanged life of man,

Is not the womb the source from which the Word began?

FIRST SUNDAY AFTER EASTER

Epistle JOHN 5:4—10

Gospel JOHN 20:19-31

19   Now when it was late that same day, the first of the week, and the doors were shut, where the disciples were gathered together, for fear of the Jews, Jesus came and stood in the midst and said to them: Peace be to you.

20   And when he had said this, he shewed them his hands and his side. The disciples therefore were glad, when they saw the Lord.

21   He said therefore to them again: Peace be to you. As the Father hath sent me, I also send you.

22   When he had said this, he breathed on them; and he said to them: Receive ye the Holy Ghost.

23   Whose sins you shall forgive, they are forgiven them: and whose sins you shall retain, they are retained.

24   Now Thomas, one of the twelve, who is called Didymus, was not with them when Jesus came.

25   The other disciples therefore said to him: We have seen the Lord. But he said to them: Except I shall see in his hands the print of the nails and put my finger into place of the nails and put my hand into his side, I will not believe.

26   And after eight days, gain his disciples were within, and Thomas with them. Jesus cometh, the doors being shut, and stood in the midst and said: Peace be to you.

27   Then he said to Thomas: Put in thy finger hither and see my hands. And bring hither thy hand and put it into my side. And be not faithless, but believing.

28   Thomas answered and said to him: My Lord and my God.

29   Jesus saith to him: Because thou hast seen me, Thomas, thou hast believed: blessed are they that have not seen and have believed.

30   Many other signs also did Jesus in the sight of his disciples, which are not written in this book.

31   But these are written, that you may believe that Jesus is the Christ, the Son of God: and that believing, you may have life in his name.

XXI

FIRST SUNDAY AFTER EASTER

The darkness of my tomb is nailed with doubt,

The shadow, barring light that truth reveals;

Within the void no blood, no waters spout

To flow, the witness that the Spirit seals.

And when the fingers on the wounds print proof

Of rising fire burning on five sides,

Above the blackness lifts the sighted roof,

And light within the death of doubt resides.

The knowledge of the Word contains no pacts

Of written wills; where honor is the seer,

Eternity demands no artifacts

To show it was and is forever here.

If sainted were the men, the twelve who saw and did believe,

Were not more blest the women, who saw not, but did believe?

XXI

SECOND SUNDAY AFTER EASTER

Epistle 1 PETER 2:21–25

21   For unto this are you called: because Christ also suffered for us, leaving you an example that you should follow his steps.

22   Who did no sin, neither was guile found in his mouth.

23   Who, when he was reviled, did not revile: when he suffered, he threatened not, but delivered himself to him that judged him unjustly.

24   Who his own self bore our sins in his body upon the tree: that we, being dead to sins, should live to justice: by whose stripes you were healed.

25   For you were as sheep going astray: but you are now converted to the shepherd and bishop of your souls.

Gospel JOHN 10:11–16

11   I am the good shepherd. The good shepherd giveth his life for his sheep.

12   But the hireling and he that is not the shepherd, whose own the sheep are not, seeth the wolf coming and leaveth the sheep and flieth: and the wolf catcheth and scattereth the sheep.

13   And the hireling flieth, because he is a hireling: and he hath no care for the sheep.

14   I am the good shepherd: and I know mine, and mine know me.

15   As the Father knoweth me, and I know the Father: and I lay down my life for my sheep.

16   And other sheep I have that are not of this fold: them also I must bring. And they shall hear my voice: and there shall be one fold and one shepherd.

SECOND SUNDAY AFTER EASTER

I need the discipline to turn my cheek,

Reviling not the demon who reviles;

And while the tree of death I daily seek,

I must not hang by words of mouth which guiles.

This sacrifice returns the straying sheep

Back to the shepherd dying for his fold;

For in deceit the hireling fawns to weep,

While to the wolf he gives his charge for gold.

"I am the only shepherd," says the Word,

"And all the sheep must come within this fold,

And only one the voice from God is heard

While breaking bread that may the wine enfold."

But, who shall say for all among the voices of the herd

Which IS the only one to bear the message of the Word?

XXII

THIRD SUNDAY AFTER EASTER

Epistle 1 PETER 2:11–19

11   Dearly beloved, I beseech you, as stranger and pilgrims, to refrain yourselves from carnal desires which war against the soul,

12   Having your conversation good among the Gentiles: that whereas they speak against you as evildoers, they may, by the good works which they shall behold in you, glorify God in the day of visitation.

13   Be ye subject therefore to every human creature for God's sake; whether it be to the king as excelling,

14   Or to governors as sent by him for the punishment of evildoers and for the praise of the good.

15   For so is the will of God, that by doing well you may put to silence the ignorance of foolish men:

Gospel JOHN 16:16-22

16   A little while, and now you shall not see me: and again a little while, and you shall see me: because I go to the Father.

17

he saith to us: A little while, and you shall not see me; and again a little while, and you shall see me, and, Because I go to the Father?

18   They said therefore: What is this that he saith, A little while? We know not what he speaketh.

19   And Jesus knew that they had a mind to ask him. And he said to them: Of this do you inquire among yourselves, because I said: A little while, and you shall not see me; and again a little while, and you shall see me?

20   Amen, amen, I say to you, that you shall lament and weep, but the world shall rejoice: and you shall be made sorrowful, but your sorrow shall be turned into joy.

21   A woman, when she is in labour, hath sorrow, because her hour is come; but when she hath brought forth the child, she remembereth no more the anguish, for joy that a man is born into the world.

22   So also you now indeed have sorrow: but I will see you again and your heart shall rejoice. And your joy no man shall take from you.

XXIII

THIRD SUNDAY AFTER EASTER

I crave the while to bear adversity,

To ripen sleeping seeds in fallen fruit,

When storms have broken branches over me

And raped the harvest for the satyred brute.

I fight to curb this flesh which daily burns

In war against the soul. The pagan sees

My blossoms in his path, and then he turns

His slander to the worship of the trees.

"What is this little while on which he speaks?"

The anguish parturition stills in birth,

Rejoicing man beyond forgotten shrieks,

Now bursts the seed once more upon the earth.

As doubt must see the sights on truth beyond
   the earth-bound tomb
Does not the little while gestate within the woman's womb?

FOURTH SUNDAY AFTER EASTER

Epistle JAMES 1:17–21

17 Every best gift and every perfect gift is from above, coming down from the Father of lights, with whom there is no change nor shadow of alteration.

19 You know, my dearest brethren. And let every man be swift to hear, but slow to speak and slow to anger.

20 For the anger of man worketh not the justice of God.

21 Wherefore, casting away all uncleanness and abundance of naughtiness, with meekness receive the ingrafted word, which is able to save your souls.

Gospel JOHN 16:5–14

5 But I told you not these things from the beginning, because I was with you. And now I go to him that sent me, and none of you asketh me: Whither goest thou?

6 But because I have spoken these things to you, sorrow hath filled your heart.

7 But I tell you the truth: it is expedient to you that I go. For if I go not, the Paraclete will not come to you: but if I go, I will send him to you.

8 And when he is come, he will convince the world of sin and of justice and of judgment.

9 Of sin: because they believed not in me.

10 And of justice: because I go to the Father: and you shall see me no longer.

11 And of judgment: because the prince of this world is already judged.

12 I have yet many things to say to you: but you cannot bear them now.

13 But when he, the Spirit of truth, is come, he will teach you all truth. For he shall not speak of himself: But what things soever he shall hear, he shall speak. And the things that are to come, he shall shew you.

14 He shall glorify me: because he shall receive of mine and shall shew it to you.

XXIV

FOURTH SUNDAY AFTER EASTER

To justice now a canticle I sing;

Be swift to hear, and slow to speak, and slow

To wrath, since wrath for justice does not bring

A scale by which the balanced tune will show.

The man, who has, must leave his goods to store,

To fill the advocate, the chore of will,

Like music makers who must work the score

That symphonies may empty chambers fill.

The "has-not" dreams of things but will not bear

The burden groaning with the price of growth;

So he who gives and he who takes must share

The scales that orchestrate the song of both.

But, why must those who sit and satiate the now

Be clapped to glory by my sweat-taxed hands and brow?

FIFTH SUNDAY AFTER EASTER

Epistle JAMES 1:22–27

22 But be ye doers of the word and not hearers only, deceiving your own selves.

23 For if a man be a hearer of the word and not a doer, he shall be compared to a man beholding his own countenance in a glass.

24 For he beheld himself and went his way and presently forgot what manner of man he was.

25 But he that hath looked into the perfect law of liberty and hath continued therein, not becoming a forgetful hearer but a doer of the work: this man shall be blessed in his deed.

26 And if any man think himself to be religious, not bridling his tongue but deceiving his own heart, this man's religion is vain.

27 Religion clean and undefiled before God and the Father is this: to visit the fatherless and widows in their tribulation and to keep one's self unspotted from this world.

Gospel JOHN 16:23–30

23 And in that day you shall not ask me any thing. Amen, amen, I say to you: if you ask the Father any thing in my name, he will give it you.

24 Hitherto, you have not asked any thing in my name. Ask, and you shall receive; that your joy may be full.

25 These things I have spoken to you in proverbs. The hour cometh when I will no more speak to you in proverbs, but will shew you plainly of the Father.

26 In that day, you shall ask in my name: and I say not to you that I will ask the Father for you.

27 For the Father himself loveth you, because you have loved me and have believed that I came out from God.

28 I came forth from the Father and am come into the world: again I leave the world and I go to the Father.

29 His disciples say to him: Behold, now thou speakest plainly and speakest no proverb.

30 Now we know that thou knowest all things and thou needest not that any man should ask thee. By this we believe that thou camest forth from God.

XXV

FIFTH SUNDAY AFTER EASTER

The metaphor is mirror of the Word

As the nightingale, the singer of the song;

And when the sound reflected is not heard,

The image is a brief and frozen wrong.

The word I hear is what in verse I do,

And put to action what my vision sees;

For what I do I am, no poet's hue;

The art itself unlocks the artist's keys.

I need no more the parable to know

What is the Word behind the author's name.

In him I find the sources from which flow

The symbols where all meanings are the same.

But, who can say which sex in symbol was the primal clod

To make what later was the scripted image of our God?

XXVI

SUNDAY AFTER the ASCENSION

Epistle 1 PETER 4:7—11

7   But the end of all is at hand. Be prudent therefore and watch in prayers.

8   But before all things have a constant mutual charity among yourselves: for charity covereth a multitude of sins.

9   Using hospitality one towards another without murmuring.

10   As every man hath received grace, ministering the same one to another, as good stewards of the manifold grace of God.

11   If any man speak, let him speak, as the words of God. If any minister, let him do it, as of the power which God administereth: that in all things God may be honoured through Jesus Christ: to whom is glory and empire for ever and ever. Amen.

Gospel JOHN 15:26-27; 16, 1—4

26   But when the Paraclete cometh, whom I will send you from the Father, the Spirit of truth, who proceedeth from the Father, he shall give testimony of me.   27   And you shall give testimony, because you are with me from the beginning.

1   These things have I spoken to you, that you may not be scandalized.

2   They will put you out of the synagogues: yea, the hour cometh, that whosoever killeth you will think that he doth a service to God.

3   And these things will they do to you; because they have not known the Father nor me.

4   But these things I have told you, that when the hour shall come, you may remember that I told you of them.

SUNDAY WITHIN OCTAVE OF ASCENSION

The one who kills me thinks he acts in love,

Not knowing of the well-spring of my prayers;

Since from my hand he sees in flight no dove

And of my garment knows no one who shares.

My wine must not stand useless hour by hour

As though the cellar door were death's stale shroud;

The sweetness of the elixir will sour

Unless it bears a witness in the crowd.

Now, from the temple was I late expelled;

My enemy surpasses me, I heard;

Although to truth my ecstacy I held

And spoke as witness to the inner Word.

Why, then, with all the promise to remember me,

Am I so scandalized beyond identity?

PENTECOST SUNDAY

Epistle ACTS 2:1—11

Gospel JOHN 14:23—31

23   Jesus answered and said to him: If any one love me, he will keep my word. And my Father will love him: and we will come to him and will make our abode with him.

24   He that loveth me not keepeth not my words. And the word which you have heard is not mine; but the Father's who sent me.

25   These things have I spoken to you, abiding with you.

26   But the Paraclete, the Holy Ghost, whom the Father will send in my name, he will teach you all things and bring all things to your mind, whatsoever I shall have said to you.

27   Peace I leave with you: my peace I give unto you: not as the world giveth, do I give unto you. Let not your heart be troubled: nor let it be afraid.

28   You have heard that I said to you: I go away, and I come unto you. If you loved me, you would indeed be glad, because I go to the Father: for the Father is greater than I.

29   And now I have told you before it come to pass: that when it shall come to pass, you may believe.

30   I will not now speak many things with you. For the prince of this world cometh: and in me he hath not any thing.

31   But that the world may know that I love the Father: and as the Father hath given me commandments, so do I. Arise, let us go hence.

XXVII

PENTECOST SUNDAY

My inner thoughts must galvanize to act,

As tongues of fire forge me to the Word

Where foreign sounds with crowds the house have packed,

Yet each the other's spirit's hum has heard.

The Word is not the speaker's gold to spin

Nor wordly matter for the prince to hoard;

As art is greater than the artist's din,

The war is longer than the warrior's sword.

Not as the world gives, do I give to you

Of peace, for, "Father greater is than I."

And I am only one of all who do

For you the things that more than dreams live by.

But, if the spirit of the truth no single language knows,

Why does one epic claim the only verses to the rose?

XXVIII

TRINITY SUNDAY

Epistle ROMANS 11:33—36

33   O the depth of the riches of the wisdom and of the knowledge of God! How incomprehensible are his judgments, and how unsearchable his ways!

34   For who hath known the mind of the Lord? Or who hath been his counsellor?

35   Or who hath first given to him, and recompense shall be made to him?

36   For of him, and by him, and in him, are all things: to him be glory for ever. Amen.

Gospel MATTHEW 28:18—20

18   And Jesus coming, spoke to them, saying: All power is given to me in heaven and in earth.

19   Going therefore, teach ye all nations: baptizing them in the name of the Father and of the Son and of the Holy Ghost.

20   Teaching them to observe all things whatsoever I have commanded you. And behold I am with you all days, even to the consummation of the world.

XXVIII

TRINITY SUNDAY

How finite is my note within the score

So infinite. This symphony of sound

Is various and always new and more

Than I can sing because my chords are bound.

The three dimensions of the song arrange

The harmonies of single measures sung;

From mind, through matter, unto spirit change

The parts on which a single theme is hung.

"Go forth and teach" that others, too, might hear;

Remove the speck that blinds the eyes to see;

Now touch away your brother's fence of fear,

And triply consummate the love in me.

But, why must I be constant as the maker of the dream?

I, too, am drumming rhythms to counterpoint the theme.

CORPUS CHRISTI

Epistle 1 CORINTHIANS 11:23–29

23   For I have received of the Lord that which also I delivered unto you, that the Lord Jesus, the same night in which he was betrayed, took bread,

24   And giving thanks, broke and said: Take ye and eat: This is my body, which shall be delivered for you. This do for the commemoration of me.

25   In like manner also the chalice, after he had supped, saying: This chalice is the new testament in my blood. This do ye, as often as you shall drink, for the commemoration of me.

26   For as often as you shall eat this bread and drink the chalice, you shall shew the death of the Lord, until he come.

27   Therefore, whosoever shall eat this bread, or drink the chalice of the Lord unworthily, shall be guilty of the body and of the blood of the Lord.

28   But let a man prove himself: and so let him eat of that bread and drink of the chalice.

29   For he that eateth and drinketh unworthily eateth and drinketh judgment to himself, not discerning the body of the Lord.

Gospel JOHN 6:56–59

56   For my flesh is meat indeed: and my blood is drink indeed.

57   He that eateth my flesh and drinketh my blood abideth in me: and I in him.

58   As the living Father hath sent me, and I live by the Father: so he that eateth me, the same also shall live by me.

59   This is the bread that came down from heaven. Not as your fathers did eat manna and are dead. He that eateth this bread shall live forever.

XXIX

CORPUS CHRISTI

I eat the bread to labor with my prose

And drink the wine to lift with poetry;

But in each change in effort I must lose

What I appear, that I may really be.

The honey from the rock, the fat of wheat,

Are food to flesh the body in the world;

But when I need above what I can eat

I must have drink that from the vine was bled.

If, worthy of the bread and of the wine,

My memory celebrates what I have heard,

I am transcended over what is mine

For transubstantiation is the Word.

Communion, then, is lifting over self to infinite;

Why need the ritual be always strict and definite?

SECOND SUNDAY AFTER PENTECOST

Epistle JOHN 3:13—18

13 Wonder not, brethren, if the world hate you.

14 We know that we have passed from death to life, because we love the brethren. He that loveth not abideth in death.

15 Whosoever hateth his brother is a murderer. And you know that no murderer hath eternal life abiding in himself.

16 In this we have known the charity of God, because he hath laid down his life for us: and we ought to lay down our lives for the brethren.

18 My little children, let us not love in word nor in tongue, but in deed and in truth.

Gospel LUKE 14:16—24

16 But he said to him: A certain man made a great supper and invited many.

17 And he sent his servant at the hour of supper to say to them that were invited, that they should come: for now all things are ready.

18 And they began all at once to make excuse. The first said to him: I have bought a farm and I must needs go out and see it. I pray thee, hold me excused.

19 And another said: I have bought five yoke of oxen and I go to try them. I pray, hold me excused.

20 And another said: I have married a wife; and therefore I cannot come.

21 And the servant returning, told these things to his lord. Then the master of the house, being angry, said to his servant: Go out quickly into the streets and lanes of the city; and bring in hither the poor and the feeble and the blind and the lame.

22 And the servant said: Lord, it is done as thou hast commanded; and yet there is room.

23 And the Lord said to the servant: Go out into the highways and hedges, and compel them to come in, that my house may be filled.

24 But I say unto you that none of those men that were invited shall taste of my supper.

XXX

SECOND SUNDAY AFTER PENTECOST

My peers compete and will not dine with me,

And yet the Word says not to be surprised;

For he who hates his brethren will not see

His power either tenured or advised.

Therefore, I sacrifice my place for him

Who undermines my life-long work and name;

Because he is a murderer, and dim

Within the fences of his life dies fame.

So none, whom I invite, my food shall taste,

Preferring farm, or oxen, wife, or shame;

Though with my betters nothing goes to waste,

I lure the poor, the crippled, blind, and lame.

Why, then, am I commanded that my brother I must love

While he with victory both hates and gloats, and all approve?

THIRD SUNDAY AFTER PENTECOST

Epistle 1 PETER 5:6–11

6   Be you humbled therefore under the mighty hand of God, that he may exalt you in the time of visitation:

7   Casting all your care upon him, for he hath care of you.

8   Be sober and watch: because your adversary the devil, as a roaring lion, goeth about seeking whom he may devour.

10   But the God of all grace, who hath called us into his eternal glory in Christ Jesus, after you have suffered a little, will himself perfect you and confirm you and establish you.

11   To him be glory and empire, for ever and ever. Amen.

Gospel LUKE 15:1–10

1   Now the publicans and sinners drew near unto him to hear him.

2   And the Pharisèes and the scribes murmured, saying: This man receiveth sinners and eateth with them.

3   And he spoke to them this parable, saying:

4   What man of you that hath an hundred sheep, and if he shall lose one of them, doth he not leave the ninety-nine in the desert and go after that which was lost, until he find it?

5   And when he hath found it, lay it up on his shoulders, rejoicing?

6   And coming home,call together his friends and neighbours, saying to them: Rejoice with me, because I have found my sheep that was lost?

7   I say to you that even so there shall be joy in heaven upon one sinner that doth penance, more than upon ninety-nine just who need not penance.

8   Or what woman having ten groats, if she lose one groat, doth not light a candle and sweep the house and seek diligently until she find it?

9   And when she hath found it, call together her friends and neighbours, saying: Rejoice with me, because I have found the groat which I had lost.

10   So I say to you, there shall be joy before the angels of God upon one sinner doing penance.

THIRD SUNDAY AFTER PENTECOST

The lion roars for someone to devour;

He stalks me like a sheep upon a plain,

And I must watch him tail-gate by the hour

My every loss which may become his gain.

I, threatened, find me all alone and poor.

Abjection and my labor bear me down,

Below the level of perfection's door

That opens to the safety of the town.

I hear one lost is welcomed with more joy

Than ninety-nine who go the charted way,

And one lost drachma more than ten is ploy

To usher in the one who cannot pay.

But, Why? What sort of town is this which is a waiting host

More grateful to one debtor than to all who've paid the cost?

XXXII

FOURTH SUNDAY AFTER PENTECOST

Epistle ROMANS 8:18—23

Gospel LUKE 5:1—11

1   And it came to pass, that when the multitudes pressed upon him to hear the word of God, he stood by the lake of Genesareth,

2   And saw two ships standing by the lake: but the fishermen were gone out of them and were washing their nets.

3   And going into one of the ships that was Simon's, he desired him to draw back a little from the land. And sitting, he taught the multitudes out of the ship.

4   Now when he had ceased to speak, he said to Simon: Launch out into the deep and let down your nets for a draught.

5   And Simon answering said to him: Master, we have laboured all the night and have taken nothing: but at thy word I will let down the net.

6   And when they had done this, they enclosed a very great multitude of fishes: and their net broke.

7   And they beckoned to their partners that were in the other ship, that they should come and help them. And they came and filled both the ships, so that they were almost sinking.

8   Which when Simon Peter saw, he fell down at Jesus' knees, saying: Depart from me, for I am a sinful man, O Lord.

9   For he was wholly astonished, and all that were with him, at the draught of the fishes which they had taken.

10   And so were also James and John the sons of Zebedee, who were Simon's partners. And Jesus saith to Simon: Fear not: from henceforth thou shalt catch men.

11   And having brought their ships to land, leaving all things, they followed him.

70

XXXII

FOURTH SUNDAY AFTER PENTECOST

The substance of creation groans in pain,

For matter burdens nets with heavy weight,

Which must break down and lose what they contain

In order to take passage at the gate.

There at Genesareth are moved the boats,

Both emptied of corrupted catch at night,

When into one the Word with key-note floats

And loads the carriers with echoed might.

"Henceforth" . . . "catch men," to leave the fruited freight,

Compress the oil, and then ferment the wine.

The boats are left upon the land to wait

While vineyards blow the song beyond the brine.

Why, then, if I put out with nets into the deep,

Am I condemned and told to ease myself with sleep?

FIFTH SUNDAY AFTER PENTECOST

Epistle 1 PETER 3:8—15

8   And in fine, be ye all of one mind, having compassion one of another, being lovers of the brotherhood, merciful, modest, humble:

9   Not rendering evil for evil, nor railing for railing, but contrariwise, blessing: for unto this re you called, that you may inherit a blessing.

10   For he that will love life and see good days, let him refrain his tongue from evil, and his lips that they speak no guile.

11   Let him decline from evil and do good: let him seek after peace and pursue it:

12   Because the eyes of the Lord are upon the just, and his ears unto their prayers: but the countenance of the Lord upon them that do evil things.

13   And who is he that can hurt you, if you be zealous of good?

14   But if also you suffer any thing for justice' sake, blessed are ye. And be not afraid of their fear: and be not troubled.

15   But sanctify the Lord Christ in your hearts, being ready always to satisfy every one that asketh you a reason of that hope which is in you.

Gospel MATTHEW 5:20—24

20   For I tell you, that unless your justice abound more than that of the scribes and Pharisees, you shall not enter into the kingdom of heaven.

21   You have heard that it was said to them of old: Thou shalt not kill. And whosoever shall kill shall be in danger of the judgment.

22   But I say to you that whosoever is angry with his brother shall be in danger of the judgment. And whosoever shall say to his brother, Raca, shall be in danger of the council. And whosoever shall say, Thou fool, shall be in danger of hell fire.

23   If therefore thou offer thy gift at the altar, and there thou remember that thy brother hath any thing against thee:

24   Leave there thy offering before the altar and go first to be reconciled to thy brother: and then coming thou shalt offer thy gift.

XXXIII

FIFTH SUNDAY AFTER PENTECOST

I fear the fear the other has of me,

Who lifts his hand to strike my offered cheek.

There is no reason why my enemy

Insist he will in me no friendship seek.

"Turn away from evil and do good," you say;

The Word speaks not for those who evil do.

They smoke the eyes of justice in their way,

While in the path of blood their course pursue.

Raged "Raca" brings a judgment on the head

Of anger paid in silver at the stone;

Before the altar gifts one bears instead

The tools for love that must his judgment hone.

But, why must I, alone, drink deeply of humility

While my victorious enemy spurs gifts and amnesty?

73

XXXIV

SIXTH SUNDAY AFTER PENTECOST

Epistle ROMANS 6:3—11

Gospel MARK 8:1—9

1   In those days again, when there was a great multitude and they had nothing to eat; calling his disciples together, he saith to them:

2   I have compassion on the multitude, for behold they have now been with me three days and have nothing to eat.

3   And if I shall send them away fasting to their home, they will faint in the way: for some of them came from afar off.

4   And his disciples answered him: From whence can any one fill them here with bread in the wilderness?

5   And he asked them: How many loaves have ye? Who said: Seven.

6   And he commanded the people to sit down on the ground. And taking the seven loaves, giving thanks, he broke and gave to his disciples for to set before them. And they set them before the people.

7   And they had a few little fishes: and he blessed them and commanded them to be set before them.

8   And they did eat and were filled: and they took up that which was left of the fragments, seven baskets.

9   And they that had eaten were about four thousand. And he sent them away.

XXXIV

SIXTH SUNDAY AFTER PENTECOST

The rose does not exude its scent in vain,

For it perfumes what was the fetid air;

Polluted particles were felled by rain

While empty atoms stood and waited there.

The washing of defilement is the food

That increments while it replaces void;

So death for sin is made alive by good,

And flowers where the seed had seemed destroyed.

And so within the desert seven-fold

The wafted wealth disseminates the crowd;

It penetrates the self; it shares the gold,

And from the body lifts the binding shroud.

If all who hunger, for compassion, eat again,

Why must I wander, famished, seeking food in vain?

SEVENTH SUNDAY AFTER PENTECOST

Epistle ROMANS 6:19—23

19   I speak an human thing, because of the infirmity of your flesh. For as you have yielded your members to serve uncleanness and iniquity, unto iniquity: so now yield your members to serve justice, unto sanctification.

20   For when you were the servants of sin, you were free men to justice.

21   What fruit therefore had you then in those things of which you are now ashamed? For the end of them is death.

22   But now being made free from sin and become servants to God, you have your fruit unto sanctification, and the end life everlasting.

23   For the wages of sin is death. But the grace of God, life everlasting in Christ Jesus our Lord.

Gospel MATTHEW 7:15—21

15 Beware of false prophets, who come to you in the clothing of sheep, but inwardly they are ravening wolves.

16   By their fruits you shall know them. Do men gather grapes of thorns, or figs of thistles?

17   Even so every good tree bringeth forth good fruit: and the evil tree bringeth forth evil fruit.

18   A good tree cannot bring forth evil fruit: neither can an evil tree bring forth good fruit.

19   Every tree that bringeth not forth good fruit shall be cut down and shall be cast into the fire.

20   Wherefore by their fruits you shall know them.

21   Not every one that saith to me, Lord, Lord, shall enter into the kingdom of heaven: but he that doth the will of my Father who is in heaven, he shall enter into the kingdom of heaven.

XXXV

SEVENTH SUNDAY AFTER PENTECOST

Trust not the liberal who hides his hate

Behind a screen of fruitless leafiness;

His rhetoric is flatulent, a bait

To catch with noise, and jam his barrenness.

As opulence enslaves, and senses die,

In justice, only, fruits of freedom live;

For wolves of passion clothe with wool the lie,

Distorting well the poison which they give.

Since by their works are known their inner seed,

(Their cry "Lord, Lord," chokes all the plants in town,

While nothing shows in harvest of a deed)

The truth is free to cut and burn them down.

But, why, in groves the wolf in any cloth ramps free,

Protected, while the rope of law entangles me?

XXXVI

EIGHTH SUNDAY AFTER PENTECOST

Epistle ROMANS 8:12–17

Gospel LUKE 16:1–9

And he said also to his disciples: There was a certain rich man who had a steward: and the same was accused unto him, that he had wasted his goods.

2　And he called him and said to him: How is it that I hear this of thee? Give an account of thy stewardship: for now thou canst be steward no longer.

3　And the steward said within himself: What shall I do, because my lord taketh away from me the stewardship? To dig I am not able; to beg I am ashamed.

4　I know what I will do, that when I shall be removed from the stewardship, they may receive me into their houses.

5　Therefore, calling together every one of his lord's debtors, he said to the first: How much dost thou owe my lord?

6　But he said: An hundred barrels of oil. And he said to him: Take thy bill and sit down quickly and write fifty.

7　Then he said to another: And how much dost thou owe? Who said: An hundred quarters of wheat. He said to him: Take thy bill and write eighty.

8　And the lord commended the unjust steward, forasmuch as he had done wisely: for the children of this world are wiser in their generation than the children of light.

9　And I say to you: Make unto you friends of the mammon of iniquity: that when you shall fail, they may receive you into everlasting dwellings.

EIGHTH SUNDAY AFTER PENTECOST

Good stewardship is prudent with demands;

It stimulates like nitrates in the soil.

It has two ends. It meets the just commands

The master makes; is wise with those who toil.

The spirit frees from bondage those who fear;

Directs them to cry "Abba" like good sons,

And each then lifts an "Ave!" as an heir

To him who asks accounting of the funds.

It does suffice to gather half the oil

The earth refunds. To ease the planter's debt

Is mammon that may other failures foil

When in the end the harvest bonds are set.

But, if the steward is unjust in plying the accounts,

Why is he given measure when he gathers by the ounce?

NINTH SUNDAY AFTER PENTECOST

Epistle 1 CORINTHIANS 10:6–13

6   Now these things were done in a figure of us, that we should not covet evil things, as they also coveted.

7   Neither become ye idolaters, as some of them, as it is written: The people sat down to eat and drink and rose up to play.

8   Neither let us commit fornication, as some of them that committed fornication: and there fell in one day three and twenty thousand.

9   Neither let us tempt Christ, as some of them tempted and perished by the serpent.

10   Neither do you murmur, as some of them murmured and were destroyed by the destroyer.

12   Wherefore, he that thinketh himself to stand, let him take heed lest he fall.

13   Let no temptation take hold on you, but such as is human. And God is faithful, who will not suffer you to be tempted above that which you are able: but will make also with temptation issue, that you may be able to bear it.

Gospel LUKE 19:41–47

41   And when he drew near, seeing the city, he wept over it, saying:

42   If thou also hadst known, and that in this thy day, the things that are to thy peace: but now they are hidden from thy eyes.

43   For the days shall come upon thee: and thy enemies shall cast a trench about thee and compass thee round and straiten thee on every side.

44   And beat thee flat to the ground, and thy children who are in thee. And they shall not leave in thee a stone upon a stone: because thou hast not known the time of thy visitation.

45   And entering into the temple, he began to cast out them that sold therein and them that bought.

46   Saying to them: It is written: My house is the house of prayer. But you have made it a den of thieves.

47   And he was teaching daily in the temple. And the chief priests and the scribes and the rulers of the people sought to destroy him.

XXXVII

NINTH SUNDAY AFTER PENTECOST

The house of prayer is not a den of thieves;

It offers not to eat nor drink nor play;

Nor does it close the door behind who leaves

His spirit there and seeks the town to fray.

Along the streets the thousand serpents lie;

The twenty-three who perished yesterday

Remind the stroller not to talk too high,

Lest he should slip where now the types decay.

The ramparts bind the rotting town and dash

The children, leaving not a stone to show,

Since he who strolled had hands of clay too rash;

He reached for gold; the height he did not know.

But, why, for more than he can grasp may man not try to reach,

If he so seeks perfection; yet for heaven he may preach?

81

XXXVIII

TENTH SUNDAY AFTER PENTECOST

Epistle 1 CORINTHIANS 12:2—11

2   You know that when you were heathens, you went to dumb idols, according as you were led.

3   Wherefore, I give you to understand that no man, speaking by the Spirit of God, saith Anathema to Jesus. And no man can say The Lord Jesus, but by the Holy Ghost.

4   Now there are diversities of graces, but the same Spirit.

5   And there are diversities of ministries, but the same Lord.

6   And there are diversities of operations, but the same God, who worketh all in all.

7   And the manifestation of the Spirit is given to every man unto profit.

8   To one indeed, by the Spirit, is given the word of wisdom: and to another, the word of knowledge, according to the same Spirit:

9   To another, faith in the same spirit: to another, the grace of healing in one Spirit.

10   To another, the working of miracles: to another prophecy:

11   But all these things, one and the same Spirit worketh, dividing to every one according as he will.

Gospel LUKE 18:9—14

9   And to some who trusted in themselves as just and despised others, he spoke also this parable:

10   Two men went up into the temple to pray: the one a Pharisee and the other a publican.

11   The Pharisee standing, prayed thus with himself: O God, I give thee thanks that I am not as the rest of men, extortioners, unjust, adulterers, as also is this publican.

12   I fast twice in a week: I give tithes of all that I possess.

13   And the publican, standing afar off, would not so much as lift up his eyes towards heaven; but struck his breast, saying: O God, be merciful to me a sinner.

14   I say to you, this man went down into his house justified rather than the other: because every one that exalteth himself shall be humbled: and he that humbleth himself shall be exalted.

XXXIX

ELEVENTH SUNDAY AFTER PENTECOST

The word is pressed as when he preached it here,

The wine of life which leavened sweat and wheat

Beyond the stone, the nightly rolling sphere;

Eleven cups were raised to toast the feat.

From Cephas to Decapolis to Rome

The sound broadcasts the rhythm of the touch;

It penetrates the sleep of those at home,

Who have no grape, but eat of flesh too much.

It vibrates to the sight of those too weak;

It opens up deaf ears to hear the sound;

And from the spittle comes the voice to speak

And free the senses man himself had bound.

But, why, at present, when the sound is lost in din,

Does not the Word define once more the death of sin?

XL

TWELFTH SUNDAY AFTER PENTECOST

Epistle 2 CORINTHIANS 3:4—9

Gospel LUKE 10:23—37

23   And turning to his disciples, he said: Blessed are the eyes that see the things which you see.

24   For I say to you that many prophets and kings have desired to see the things that you see and have not seen them; and to hear the things that you hear and have not heard them.

25   And behold a certain lawyer stood up, tempting him and saying, Master, what must I do to possess eternal life?

26   But he said to him: What is written in the law? How readest thou?

27   He answering, said: Thou shalt love the Lord thy God with thy whole heart and with thy whole soul and will all thy strength and with all thy mind: and thy neighbor as thyself.

28   And he said to him: Thou hast answered right. This do: and thou shalt live.

29   But he willing to justify himself, said to Jesus: And who is my neighbor?

30   And Jesus answering, said: A certain man went down from Jerusalem to Jericho and fell among robbers, who also stripped him and having wounded him went away, leaving him half dead.

31   And it chanced, that a certain priest went down the same way: and seeing him, passed by.

32   In like manner also a Levite, when he was near the place and saw him, passed by.

33   But a certain Samaritan, being on his journey, came near him: and seeing him, was moved with compassion:

34   And going up to him, bound up his wounds, pouring in oil and wine: and setting him upon his own beast, brought him to an inn and took care of him.

35   And the next day he took out two pence and gave to the host and said: Take care of him; and whatsoever thou shalt spend over and above, I, at my return, will repay thee.

36   Which of these three, in thy opinion, was neighbour to him that fell among the robbers?

37   But he said: He that shewed mercy to him. And Jesus said to him: Go, and do thou in like manner.

86

XL

TWELFTH SUNDAY AFTER PENTECOST

Compassion is the oil that heals the wounds,

The ministration palmed to justify.

It is the tie which holds all pain in bounds,

Renewing life for who was left to die.

Alone the letter of the word will kill;

The spirit it communicates gives life,

Just as analysis can never fill

The heart that brothers have made void with strife.

For, when among the thieves the neighbor fell,

The pitying Samaritan came by,

He sought no pedigree by which to tell

The man's belief; he would not let him die.

But, why, when I put out my hand to help my ailing friend,

He grudges me his gratitude, resents me to the end?

87

XLI

THIRTEENTH SUNDAY AFTER PENTECOST

Epistle GALATIANS 3:16-22

16   To Abraham were the promises made and to his seed. He saith not: And to his seeds, as of many. But as of one: And to thy seed, which is Christ.

17   Now this I say: that the testament which was confirmed by God, the law which was made after four hundred and thirty years doth not disannul, to make the promise of no effect.

18   For if the inheritance be of the law, it is no more of promise. But God gave it to Abraham by promise.

19   Why then was the law? It was set because of transgressions, until the seed should come to whom he made the promise, being ordained by angels in the hand of a mediator.

20   Now a mediator is not of one: but God is one.

21   Was the law then against the promises of God? God forbid! For if there had been a law given which could give life, verily justice should have been by the law.

22   But the scripture hath concluded all under sin, that the promise, by the faith of Jesus Christ, might be given to them that believe.

Gospel LUKE 17:11—19

11   And it came to pass, as he was going to Jerusalem, he passed through the midst of Samaria and Galilee.

12   And as he entered into a certain town, there met him ten men that were lepers, who stood afar off

13   And lifted up their voice, saying: Jesus Master, have mercy on us.

14   Whom when he saw, he said: Go, shew yourselves to the priests. And it came to pass, as they went, they were made clean.

15   And one of them, when he saw that he was made clean, went back, with a loud voice glorifying God.

16   And he fell on his face before his feet, giving thanks. And this was a Samaritan.

17   And Jesus answering, said: Were not ten made clean? And where are the nine?

18   There is no one found to return and give glory to God, but this stranger.

19   And he said to him: Arise, go thy way; for thy faith hath made thee whole.

THIRTEENTH SUNDAY AFTER PENTECOST

The covenant is prior to the law,

For it equates me with the promised Word.

Transgressions then discorded in the flaw

And hordes of angels sang to one who heard.

Before him ten with leprosy are ill

And each he cleanses who may then rejoice;

But only one returns with song to fill

The air with praises of a thankful voice.

The Word itself seeks echoes of its sound

And waits in chambers empty of the nine.

Ourside the scale of music he has found

A single note to give his song a line.

Why, then, in concert is it not so opportune

To give the Word for all some other measured tune?

FOURTEENTH SUNDAY AFTER PENTECOST

Epistle GALATIANS 5:16—24

Gospel MATTHEW 6:24-33

23   No man can serve two masters. For either he will hate the one and love the other: or he will sustain the one and despise the other. You cannot serve God and mammon.

25   Therefore I say to you, be not solicitous for your life, what you shall eat, nor for your body, what you shall put on. Is not the life more than the meat and the body more than the raiment?

26   Behold the birds of the air, for they neither sow, nor do they reap nor gather into barns: and your heavenly Father feedeth them. Are not you of much more value than they?

27   And which of you by taking thought can add to his stature one cubit?

28   And for raiment why are you solicitous? Consider the lilies of the field, how they grow: they labour not, neither do they spin.

29   But I say to you that not even Solomon in all his glory was arrayed as one of these.

30   And if the grass of the field, which is to-day and to-morrow is cast into the oven, God doth so clothe: how much more you, O ye of little faith?

31   Be not solicitous therefore, saying, What shall we eat: or, What shall we drink: or, Wherewith shall we be clothed?

32   For after all these things do the heathens seek. For your Father knoweth that you have need of all these things.

33   Seek ye therefore first the kingdom of God and his justice: and all these things shall be added unto you.

FOURTEENTH SUNDAY AFTER PENTECOST

You say that I two masters may not serve,

For each would claim my incense and my hand;

That in dividing parts of my preserve

In two, one would the other reprimand.

The lily needs no cloth to bear the sun

While I hug gilded garments in the snow.

The birds don't harvest, for the seeds they shun,

That I have planted, but the crop must grow.

The poor in hungry toil dream not of wine,

For when they breathe those fumes, their substance dies;

And wine alone cannot delight the soul,

For bread must line the cup wherein it lies.

But, why, if I revere you with the perfume of the rose,

May I not prime the soil that bleeds the color where it blows?

XLIII

FIFTEENTH SUNDAY AFTER PENTECOST

Epistle GALATIANS 5:25—26; 6:1—10

Gospel LUKE 7:11—16

11   And it came to pass afterwards that he went into a city that is called and there went with him his disciples and a great multitude.

12   And when he came nigh to the gate of the city, behold a dead man was carried out, the only son of his mother: and she was a widow. And a great multitude of the city was with her.

13   Whom when the Lord had seen, being moved with mercy towards her, he said to her: Weep not.

14   And he came near and touched the bier. And they that carried it stood still. And he said: Young man, I say to thee, arise.

15   And he that was dead sat up and begun to speak. And he gave him to his mother.

16   And there came a fear upon them all: and they glorified God, saying: A great prophet is risen up among us: and, God hath visited his people.

XLIII

FIFTEENTH SUNDAY AFTER PENTECOST

In crowds each one the weight of others wears

And so he lifts himself from nothingness;

For all he bears, so much the fruit he shares,

Where death would give him only barrenness.

Each is the son of woman left alone

Who leads the arid man to seed the vine;

Then, ripened, she lies flat upon the stone

And bleeds her fluid to the promised wine.

The slab is touched; the bearers all stand still

As man sits up and then begins to speak

Of love and brotherhood. So God must fill

All woman, silent with her birth-stained cheek.

As "Do not weep," the Lord the mother so advised,

Why, so reborn, must man by woman be revised?

93

XLIV

SIXTEENTH SUNDAY AFTER PENTECOST

Epistle EPHESIANS 3:13–21

Gospel LUKE 14:1-11

1   And it came to pass, when Jesus went into the house of one of the chief of the Pharisees, on the sabbath day, to eat bread, that they watched him.

2   And behold, there was a certain man before him that had the dropsy.

3   And Jesus answering, spoke to the lawyers and Pharisees, saying: Is it lawful to heal on the sabbath day?

4   But they held their peace. But he taking him, healed him and sent him away.

5   And answering them, he said: Which of you shall have an ass or an ox fall into a pit and will not immediately draw him out, on the sabbath day?

6   And they could not answer him to these things.

7   And he spoke a parable also to them that were invited, marking how they chose the first seats at the table, saying to them:

8   When thou art invited to a wedding, sit not down in the first place, lest perhaps one more honourable than thou be invited by him:

9   And he that invited thee and him, come and say to thee: Give this man place. And then thou begin with shame to take the lowest place.

10   But when thou art invited, go, sit down in the lowest place; that when he who invited thee cometh, he may say to thee: Friend, go up higher. Then shalt thou have glory before them that sit at table with thee.

11   Because every one that exalteth himself shall be humbled: and he that humbleth himself shall be exalted.

SIXTEENTH SUNDAY AFTER PENTECOST

No knowledge is so wide and deep as love,

You say; that faith both roots and grounds the man

With inner reach beyond the quest above,

To branch more power than the loveless can;

That this ripe man must not at right recline

To place him next the giver of the feast;

And woman must from any place decline,

For ruling man has tied her to the beast.

The invitation promises a place

Much higher than a gilded stolen seat;

With gold the power thief cannot fill space

Where grape is wine and bread replaces wheat.

But, what of frauds who fashion failures into victories,

Presenting generals as fools and kings in parodies?

XLV

SEVENTEENTH SUNDAY AFTER PENTECOST

Epistle EPHESIANS 4:1—6

1   I therefore, a prisoner in the Lord, beseech you that you walk worthy of the vocation in which you are called:

2   With all humility and mildness, with patience, supporting one another in charity.

3   Careful to keep the unity of the Spirit in the bond of peace.

4   One body and one Spirit: as you are called in one hope of your calling.

5   One Lord, one faith, one baptism.

6   One God and Father of all, who is above all, and through all, and in us all.

Gospel MATTHEW 22:34-46

34   But the Pharisees, hearing that he had silenced the Sadducees, came together.

35   And one of them, a doctor of the law, asked him, tempting him:

36   Master, which is the great commandment in the law?

37   Jesus said to him: Thou shalt love the Lord thy God with thy whole heart and with thy whole soul, and with thy whole mind.

38   This is the greatest and the first commandment.

39   And the second is like to this: Thou shalt love thy neighbour as thyself.

40   On these two commandments dependeth the whole law and the prophets.

41   And the Pharisees being gathered together, Jesus asked them,

42   Saying: What think you of Christ? Whose son is he? They say to him: David's.

43   He saith to them: How then doth David in spirit call him Lord, saying:

44   The Lord said to my Lord: Sit on my right hand, until I make thy enemies thy footstool?

45   If David then call him Lord, how is he his son?

46   And no man was able to answer him a word: neither durst any man from that day forth ask him any more questions.

96

SEVENTEENTH SUNDAY AFTER PENTECOST

The unity of God is gold of peace,

The banner, dream, the vision, record, truth.

The wise of Rome, the Orient, and Greece,

All fleshed this fort, despite the pirate youth

Who burned the log, the captain's ship, the wand;

Yet, ageless enemy, he aped the breed.

To love the neighbor is the old command;

It tells us not his nation, sex, or creed.

As in the autumn stands the bared oak's rod,

Without the vine that one had couched its seed,

The tree is neither soil, nor host, nor pod;

It is the fruit that human love decreed.

But, why must I make wine from vines my neighbors see,

If they for bread are sly and hide my enemy?

EIGHTEENTH SUNDAY AFTER PENTECOST

Epistle 1 CORINTHIANS 1:4-8

4   I give thanks to my God always for you, for the grace of God that is given you in Christ Jesus:

5   That in all things you are made rich in him, in all utterance and in all knowledge.

6   As the testimony of Christ was confirmed in you,

7   So that nothing is wanting to you in any grace, waiting for the manifestation of our Lord Jesus Christ.

8   Who also will confirm you unto the end without crime, in the days of the coming of our Lord Jesus Christ.

Gospel MATTHEW 9:1-8

And entering into a boat, he passed over the water and came into his own city.

2   And behold they brought to him one sick of the palsy lying in a bed. And Jesus, seeing their faith, said to the man sick of the palsy: Be of good heart, son. Thy sins are forgiven.

3   And behold some of the scribes said within themselves: He blasphemeth.

4   And Jesus seeing their thoughts, said: Why do you think evil in your hearts?

5   Whether is easier, to say. Thy sins are forgiven thee: or to say, Arise, and walk?

6   But that you may know that the Son of man hath power on earth to forgive sins, (then said he to the man sick of the palsy): Arise, take up thy bed and go into thy house.

7   And he arose and went into his house.

8   And the multitude seeing it, feared, and glorified God that gave such power to men.

XLVI

EIGHTEENTH SUNDAY AFTER PENTECOST

The mind of man unlocks the spring of grace;

There flow all utterance and knowledge bred

In God, like water brooking every trace

To sea, below the level of the shed.

The infant ground-spring is all clarity

With morning peace, and promises to make

The mud-slushed rivers reach maturity

And from perfection let redemption break.

But rain-parched streams that race the evening star

Are paralytics framed within a bed;

Their onward course may only flow so far

As where all other streams to sea have led.

Why must I help my neighbor rise and walk to town,

Wrapped in my mat which he by lies has made his own?

99

XLVII

NINETEENTH SUNDAY AFTER PENTECOST

Epistle EPHESIANS 4:23–28

23   And be renewed in the spirit of your mind.

24   And put on the new man, who according to God is created in justice and holiness of truth.

25   Wherefore, putting away lying, speak ye the truth, every man with his neighbor. For we are members one of another.

26   Be angry: and sin not. Let not the sun go down upon your anger.

27   Give not place to the devil.

28   He that stole, let him now steal no more: but rather let him labour, working with his hands the thing which is good, that he may have something to give to him that suffereth need.

Gospel MATTHEW 22:1–14

1   And Jesus answering, spoke again in parables to them, saying:

2   The kingdom of heaven is likened to a king who made a marriage for his son.

3   And he sent his servants to call them that were invited to the marriage: and they would not come.

4   Again he sent other servants, saying: Tell them that were invited. Behold, I have prepared my dinner; my beeves and fatlings are killed, and all things are ready. Come ye to the marriage.

5   But they neglected and went their ways, one to his farm and another to his merchandise.

6   And the rest laid hands on his servants and, having treated them contumeliously, put them to death.

7   But when the king had heard of it, he was angry: and sending his armies, he destroyed those murderers and burnt their city.

8   Then he saith to his servants: The marriage indeed is ready; but they that were invited were not worthy.

9   Go ye therefore into the highways; and as many as you shall find, call to the marriage.

10   And his servants going forth into the ways, gathered together all that they found, both bad and good: and the marriage was filled with guests.

11   And the king went in to see the guests: and he saw there a man who had not on a wedding garment.

12   And he saith to him: Friend, how camest thou in hither not having on a wedding garment? But he was silent.

13   Then the king said to the waiters: Bind his hands and feet, and cast him into the exterior darkness. There, shall be weeping and gnashing of teeth.

14   For many are called, but few are chosen.

NINETEENTH SUNDAY AFTER PENTECOST

I wear the proper thing for what I do,

The shreds for garden fray, the frills for play.

The dress is for the place that I go to;

It fits the scene and suits the night or day.

Before my friend I put away the lie,

The anger of discord that steals his love;

And for his vision tint the pleasing dye,

So, clothed in truth, together we may rove;

As servants we attend the marriage feast

Where those who were invited do not come,

And those with wedding garments are the least,

The chosen, while the most are cast to roam.

But, why am I, unknown, thus called to come at all

If I no garment own to grace a banquet hall?

XLVIII

TWENTIETH SUNDAY AFTER PENTECOST

Epistle EPHESIANS 5:15-21

15   See therefore, brethren, how you walk circumspectly: not as unwise,

16   But as wise: redeeming the time, because the days are evil.

17   Wherefore, becoming not unwise: but understanding what is the will of God.

18   And be not drunk with wine, wherein is luxury: but be ye filled with the holy Spirit,

19   Speaking to yourselves in psalms and hymns and spiritual canticles, singing and making melody in your hearts to the Lord:

20   Giving thanks always for all things, in the name of our Lord Jesus Christ, to God and the Father:

21   Being subject one to another, in the fear of Christ.

Gospel JOHN 4:46-53

46   He came again therefore into Cana of Galilee, where he made the water wine. And there was a certain ruler, whose son was sick at Capharnaum.

47   He having heard that Jesus was come from Judea into Galilee, went to him and prayed him to come down and heal his son: for he was at the point of death.

48   Jesus therefore said to him: Unless you see signs and wonders, you believe not.

49   The ruler saith to him: Lord, come down before that my son die.

50   Jesus saith to him: Go thy way. Thy son liveth. The man believed the word which Jesus said to him and went his way.

51   And as he was going down, his servants met him: and they brought word, saying, that his son lived.

52   He asked therefore of them the hour wherein he grew better. And they said to him: Yesterday, at the seventh hour, the fever left him.

53   The Father therefore knew that it was at the same hour that Jesus said to him: Thy son liveth. And himself believed, and his whole house.

102

XLVIII

TWENTIETH SUNDAY AFTER PENTECOST

Be careful not to drink too deep the wine;

The cup is never empty of the flow.

One sip a day brings singing to the sign

That marks the score of music you must know.

With care you walk to make the most of time,

And check the overflow of wasted days,

For in your royal bed at home your prime,

Your son, lies ill; and death a finger lays.

The simple psalm surpasses symphonies;

An hour is enough of time to speak

The Word to him who sees and then believes

That life renews where death had paled the cheek.

But, why were you so favored, you were made to see

The Word which book and faith alone have shown to me?

TWENTY-FIRST SUNDAY AFTER PENTECOST

Epistle EPHESIANS 6:10—17

Gospel MATTHEW 18:23—35

23   Therefore is the kingdom of heaven likened to a king who would take an account of his servants.

24   And when he had begun to take the account, one was brought to him that owed him ten thousand talents.

25   And as he had not wherewith to pay it, his lord commanded that he should be sold, and his wife and children and all that he had, and payment to be made.

26   But that servant falling down besought him, saying: Have patience with me and I will pay thee all.

27   And the lord of that servant, being moved with pity, let him go and forgave him the debt.

28   But when that servant was gone out, he found one of his fellow servants that owed him an hundred pence: and laying hold of him, he throttled him, saying: Pay what thou owest.

29   And his fellow servant, falling down, besought him, saying: Have patience with me and I will pay thee all.

30   And he would not: but went and cast him into prison till he paid the debt.

31   Now his fellow servants, seeing what was done, were very much grieved: and they came and told their lord all that was done.

32   Then his lord called him and said to him: Thou wicked servant, I forgave thee all the debt, because thou besoughtest me:

33   Shouldst not thou then have had compassion also on thy fellow servant, even as I had compassion on thee?

34   And his lord being angry, delivered him to the torturers until he paid all the debt.

35   So also shall my heavenly Father do to you, if you forgive not every one his brother from your hearts.

TWENTY-FIRST SUNDAY AFTER PENTECOST

To donate mercy is to fund a war;

It is a climb that must come down again.

It gifts a weapon and a locking bar;

It threatens peace, ties friendship with a chain.

The shield of faith, the breastplate justice wears

Are for the spirit armor and a sword;

And these in readiness the giver bears

To render safe the helmet of the Word.

Ten thousand talents mercy will outlive,

Releases that the servants' masters hold;

But servants, freed, in turn, do not forgive;

They stifle pity in their grasp for gold.

So, why must I my old transgressor from his debt set free,

While he, in turn, destroys all others and surpasses me?

TWENTY-SECOND SUNDAY AFTER PENTECOST

Epistle PHILIPPIANS 1:6–11

6   Being confident of this very thing: that he who hath begun a good work in you will perfect it unto the day of Christ Jesus.

7   As it is meet for me to think this for you all, for that I have you in my heart; and that, in my hands and in the defence and confirmation of the gospel, you all are partakers of my joy.

8   For God is my witness how I long after you all in the bowels of Jesus Christ.

9   And this I pray: That your charity may more and more abound in knowledge and in all understanding:

10   That you may approve the better things: that you may be sincere and without offence unto the day of Christ:

11   Filled with the fruit of justice, through Jesus Christ, unto the glory and praise of God.

Gospel MATTHEW 22:15–21

15   Then the Pharisees going, consulted among themselves how to insnare him in his speech.

16   And they sent to him their disciples with the Herodians, saying: Master, we know that thou art a true speaker and teachest the way of God in truth. Neither carest thou for any man: for thou dost not regard the person of men.

17   Tell us therefore what dost thou think? Is it lawful to give tribute to Caesar, or not?

18   But Jesus knowing their wickedness, said: Why do you tempt me, ye hypocrites?

19   Shew me the coin of the tribute. And they offered him a penny.

20   And Jesus saith to them: Whose image and inscription is this?

21   They say to him: Caesar's. Then he saith to them: Render therefore to Caesar the things that are Caesar's, and to God, the things that are God's.

TWENTY-SECOND SUNDAY AFTER PENTECOST

Discernment is the grist of charity,

Controlling like the rudder of the sail.

It holds the tack on love in ecstasy

And tempers where exaggerations fail.

The gifted things are first in knowledge bound

And then presented wrapt without offense;

The donor gives where proper need is found

And, giving, asks no craft nor mean defense.

The power of the spirit conquers all,

But could by bigness topple in the wind;

Let Caesar have one side; it will not fall,

For discipline holds love within the mind.

Why does the unleashed spirit, then, so much more now demand

What was so justly Caesar's and is now so out of hand?

TWENTY-THIRD SUNDAY AFTER PENTECOST

Epistle PHILIPPIANS 3:17—21; 4, 1—3

Gospel MATTHEW 9:18—26

18   As he was speaking these things unto them, behold a certain ruler came and adored him, saying: Lord, my daughter is even now dead; but come, lay thy hand upon her and she shall live.

19   And Jesus rising up followed him, with his disciples.

20   And behold a woman who was troubled with an issue of blood twelve years came behind him and touched the hem of his garment.

21   For she said within herself: If I shall touch only his garment, I shall be healed.

22   But Jesus turning and seeing her, said: Be of good heart, daughter. Thy faith hath made thee whole. And the woman was made whole from that hour.

23   And when Jesus was come into the house of the ruler and saw the minstrels and the multitude making a rout,

24   He said: Give place: for the girl is not dead, but sleepeth. And they laughed him to scorn.

25   And when the multitude was put forth, he went in and took her by the hand. And the maid arose.

26   And the fame hereof went abroad into all that country.

TWENTY-THIRD SUNDAY AFTER PENTECOST

Now from the depths we do not even cry;

The god that is our belly jells with fat.

We glory in our shame, so low we lie,

We honor perfidy and feed the rat.

The legal mouths of power spread their lies

With broken crosses, preaching peace to win,

While generating war. The vision dies;

The virgin sleeps as flutes play loud a din;

And with them all we crowd and laugh with scorn,

Not knowing of the sound the Word has made.

The girl may rise, her shroud be touched and torn,

But out of depths where we reflect the shade.

Why, then, must we with all this noise our senses keep

While never once are we touched out of lethal sleep?

TWENTY-FOURTH SUNDAY AFTER PENTECOST

Epistle COLOSSIANS 1:9—14

Gospel MATTHEW 24:15—35

15   When therefore you shall see the abomination of desolation, which was spoken of by Daniel the prophet, standing in the holy place: he that readeth let him understand.

16   Then they that are in Judea, let them flee to the mountains:

21   For there shall be then great tribulation, such as hath not been from the beginning of the world until now, neither shall be.

22   And unless those days had been shortened, no flesh should be saved: but for the sake of the elect those days shall be shortened.

23   Then if any man shall say to you, Lo here is Christ, or there: do not believe him.

24   For there shall arise false Christs and false prophets and shall shew great signs and wonders, insomuch as to deceive (if possible) even the elect.

25   Behold I have told it to you, beforehand.

27   For as lightning cometh out of the east and appeareth even into the west: so shall also the coming of the Son of man be.

28   Wheresoever the body shall be, there shall the eagles also be gathered together.

29   And immediately after the tribulation of those days, the sun shall be darkened and the moon shall not give her light and the stars shall fall from heaven and the powers of heaven shall be moved.

30   And then shall appear the sign of the Son of man in heaven. And then shall all tribes of the earth mourn: and they shall see the Son of man coming in the clouds of heaven with much power and majesty.

31   And he shall send his angels with a trumpet and a great voice: and they shall gather together his elect from the four winds, from the farthest parts of the heavens and the utmost bounds of them.

32   And from the fig tree learn a parable: When the branch thereof is now tender and the leaves come forth, you know that summer is nigh.

33   So you also, when you shall see all these things know ye that it is nigh, even at the doors.

34   Amen I say to you that this generation shall not pass till all these things be done.

35   Heaven and earth shall pass: but my words shall not pass.

LII

TWENTY-FOURTH SUNDAY AFTER PENTECOST

Each drama must a final curtain draw

That puts conclusion to incentive pull.

The actor who so preened the stage and saw

His fellow actors, with his art is full.

The author gives the lines for him to speak

That he reflect the words to fruits of joy,

Directing his momentum to the peak

Of mountain tops where plays no longer cloy.

There at the heights where clouds and eagles fly

Above the final darkness, light of sound,

The trumpets give the Word a gathered cry,

The cue in which eternity is found.

But, why upon this stage, unplotted and undressed,

Are all the speeches muffed and all the side-lines stressed?